What
greater gift
than the love
of a cat?

CHARLES DICKENS

ALWAYS IN MY HEART,
MY PRECIOUS CAT...

Cover and interior design by Nicole Dougherty

Artwork © 2017 Ginger Chen

CAT TALES

Copyright © 2017 by Harvest House Publishers
Published by Harvest House Publishers
Eugene, Oregon 97402
www.harvesthousepublishers.com

ISBN 978-0-7369-7145-4

Printed in China

17 18 19 20 21 22 23 24 25 / RDS-JC / 10 9 8 7 6 5 4 3 2 1

CAT TALES

HARVEST HOUSE PUBLISHERS
EUGENE, OREGON

A CAT WARMS YOUR WORLD

Nothing quite warms up a home like a cat (or two or three or more!). A cat curled up on the sofa or stretched out on the front porch swing is just so cozy and inviting. And nothing quite says relax like a cat hanging out on your lap, purring contentedly as you massage it behind the ears.

Life is just better with a cat!

Whether your cat is a tiny kitten or has been a part of your family for a long time, it's fun to capture the memories of your feline friend. Each cat has its own unique personality—the quirks and characteristics that set it apart from every other cat and make it the perfect pet for you.

Have fun writing down favorite tidbits about your cat—and don't worry about filling in the pages all at once. You can do it at cat speed—a little bit here, another part there, relaxed and completely on your own time.

And if you find a cat on your lap as soon as you sit down to fill in a few pages? Well, it goes without saying that you focus on the cat!

Time spent with a cat is never wasted.

COLETTE

ALL ABOUT
MY CAT

Name

Birthdate

Breed

Eye Color

Fur Color and Type

Other Distinguishing Marks

Did your cat enter your home as a
tiny kitten or as an older companion?
Briefly, record your cat's adoption story.

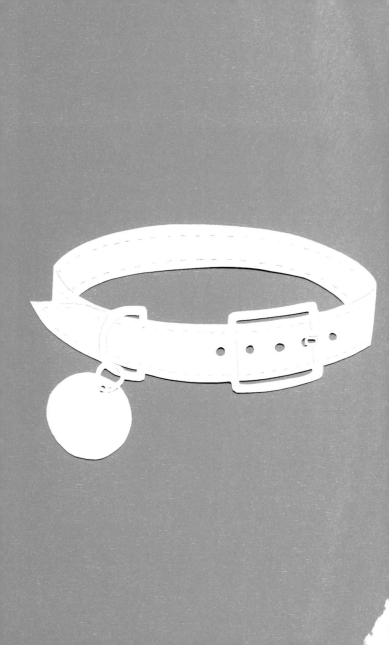

Tell the story behind your cat's name.

Describe your cat's one-of-a-kind meow.

_____

_____

_____

_____

_____

_____

_____

A LITTLE
DROWSING CAT
IS AN IMAGE
OF PERFECT
BEATITUDE.

JULES CHAMPFLEURY

Does your cat have a picky palate, or does it eat absolutely everything? Record what brand of food your feline prefers.

_____

_____

_____

_____

_____

The smallest
feline is a
masterpiece.

LEONARDO DA VINCI

What were your first impressions of
your feline? Were they accurate—or
were you in for a surprise?

How does your cat show you affection?

_____

_____

_____

_____

_____

_____

_____

Pets can give us a scare! What has your cat done that has freaked you out?

Describe the situation—and be sure to include the happy ending.

Some cats adore the companionship of fellow felines, while others prefer to fly solo. What does your cat think of other kitties?

_____

_____

_____

_____

_____

WHEN A MAN
LOVES CATS, I AM HIS
FRIEND AND COMRADE,
WITHOUT FURTHER
INTRODUCTION.

MARK TWAIN

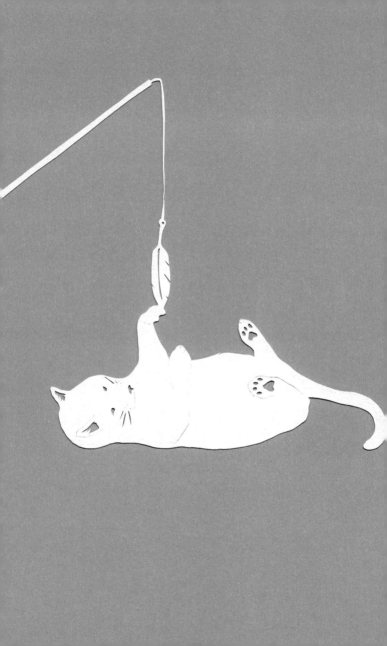

Whether it's a hand-sewn catnip mouse or a grape that has fallen onto the floor, every cat has its treasured toys. What does your cat prefer to play with?

Just like their humans, some cats
are outgoing while others are shy.
How does your cat respond to visitors?

Time for a little art therapy!
Grab some colored pencils and sketch a
drawing of your cat. Don't worry about
what it looks like. Just have fun!

Cats pop up throughout classic literature and films. Which of these cherished cats most reminds you of *your* favorite feline?

____ Dr. Seuss's *Cat in the Hat*

____ Puss in Boots

____ Beatrix Potter's Tom Kitten

____ Beatrix Potter's Miss Moppet

____ Cheshire Cat from *Alice in Wonderland*

____ C.S. Lewis's Aslan from *The Chronicles of Narnia*

____ Holly Golightly's cat—named Cat—from *Breakfast at Tiffany's*

____ Polar Bear from *The Cat Who Came for Christmas*

If your cat were
a famous figure
from history, who
would it be?

How does your cat greet you when you
arrive home from work or a day out?

A HOUSE ISN'T A HOME WITHOUT THE INEFFABLE CONTENTMENT OF A CAT WITH ITS TAIL FOLDED ABOUT ITS FEET. A CAT GIVES MYSTERY, CHARM, SUGGESTION.

L.M. MONTGOMERY, *EMILY'S QUEST*

How does your cat communicate
its happiness? Its unhappiness?

_____

_____

_____

_____

_____

_____

Write down the top ten adjectives
that characterize your cat.

1. _____

2. _____

3. _____

4. _____

5. _____

6. _____

7. _____

8. _____

9. _____

10. _____

BEHIND EVERY
great person,
THERE IS A
great cat.

ANONYMOUS

Write down all the places
your cat *loves* to scratch.

_____

_____

_____

_____

_____

_____

Confession time! Record your "pet" peeves about your cat (*lovingly, of course!*). And then write down your cat's "pet" peeves about its people.

What causes your kitty to
purr with contentment?

Paste a favorite
photo with you and
your cat here.

Or take a silly selfie together now!

What do you imagine your cat does
all day when nobody else is home?

I HAVE STUDIED
MANY PHILOSOPHERS
AND MANY CATS.
THE WISDOM OF CATS
IS INFINITELY SUPERIOR.

HIPPOLYTE TAINE

Every cat has its favorite human. Which lap (or laps) does your cat like best?

Sometimes dogs and cats are best buddies. Cats have even befriended chickens! Does your cat have any unique friendships?

Set a paper grocery bag or
a cardboard box near your cat.
Watch for a few minutes,
and then write down
how your cat responds.

_____

_____

_____

_____

_____

I LOVE THEM,
THEY ARE SO
NICE AND SELFISH.
DOGS ARE TOO
GOOD AND UNSELFISH.
THEY MAKE ME FEEL
UNCOMFORTABLE.
BUT CATS ARE
GLORIOUSLY
HUMAN.

L.M. MONTGOMERY,
ANNE OF THE ISLAND

Some cats sleep contentedly on their owner's bed. Other cats get all hyped up come sundown. Describe your cat's nocturnal habits.

Pets can be picky and persnickety!
Record a few of your feline's
peculiarities.

_____

_____

_____

_____

_____

_____

_____

Does your cat receive birthday
or Christmas presents from you?
What gifts do you give?

Describe your pet's personality
in five or fewer words...

1. _____

2. _____

3. _____

4. _____

5. _____

What's the craziest thing
your cat has done?

Hear our humble
prayer, O God.
Make us, ourselves,
to be true friends
to the animals.

ALBERT SCHWEITZER

If your cat could choose
a favorite ice cream flavor,
what do you think it would be?

_____

Above all else, I love *this*
about being a cat owner...

If you could dress your cat for a day, which clothes would you choose?

ALL THINGS
BRIGHT & BEAUTIFUL,
ALL CREATURES
GREAT & SMALL,
ALL THINGS
WISE & WONDERFUL,
THE LORD GOD
MADE THEM ALL.

CECIL ALEXANDER

Ahhhh...a feline's greatest joy is stretching out in the sun. Where is your cat's preferred place to bask?

_____

_____

_____

_____

_____

Cats can be sneaky.
When you can't seem to locate
your cat, where do you look?

WHEN A CAT
flatters...
HE IS NOT INSINCERE:
YOU MAY SAFELY
TAKE IT FOR REAL
kindness.

WALTER SAVAGE LANDOR,
IMAGINARY CONVERSATIONS

How does your cat react to
unpleasant situations—such as going
to the groomer's or being bathed?
Do you have a compliant kitty, or are
the protests heard far and wide?

_____

_____

_____

_____

_____

_____

How does your furry friend inspire you?

For Charles Dickens, Mark Twain, Louisa May Alcott, and cartoonist Jim Davis, creator of Garfield, *a beloved cat was an important part of their creative process.*

Jot down a silly kitten memory.

_____

_____

_____

_____

_____

_____

_____

_____

_____

_____

_____

_____

_____

_____

_____

_____

If we treated
everyone we meet
with the same
affection we bestow
upon our favorite
cat, they, too,
would purr.

MARTIN DELANY

If your cat
were a celebrity,
who would it be?

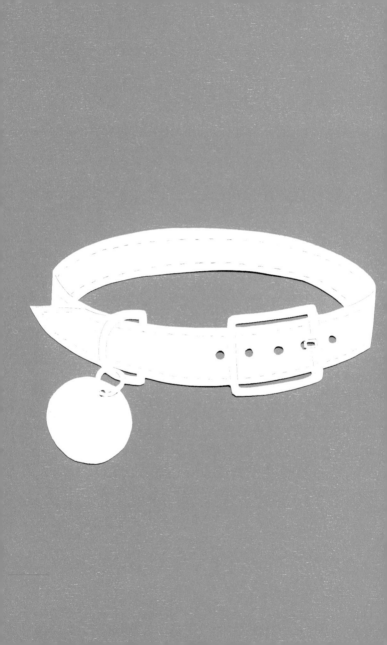

Chronicle all of your
cat's nicknames—as many
as you can think of!

_____

_____

_____

_____

_____

_____

_____

_____

_____

What does your cat do that
makes you smile?

_____

_____

_____

_____

_____

I WISH
I COULD
WRITE AS
MYSTERIOUS
AS A CAT.

EDGAR ALLAN POE

Cats can get into crazy situations—and spaces! Describe a funny place or space where you found your cat.

_____

_____

_____

_____

_____

_____

_____

Animals can often sense a storm before it arrives. How does your cat act when the weather's about to get wild?

Go ahead and admit it—you talk to your cat. (More than 95 percent of us do!) What do you like to tell your cozy companion?

_____

_____

_____

_____

_____

_____

...And what do you imagine your cat would say back to you?

When my cats
arent happy,
I'm not happy.

PERCY BYSSHE SHELLEY

If your cat is an outdoor cat, you're probably familiar with some of the "gifts" it has brought you. Write down some of those gifts here...if you dare!

What has been the most
rewarding part of owning a cat?
The most challenging part?

Is your cat a pampered pet?
Brainstorm some fun ideas for
spoiling your furry companion.

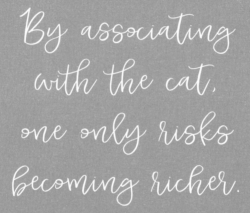

By associating
with the cat,
one only risks
becoming richer.

COLETTE

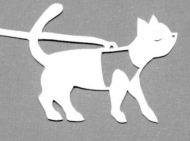

Tell the stories of *your* cat's nine lives.

1. _____

_____

_____

2. _____

_____

_____

3. _____

_____

_____

4. _____

_____

_____

5. _____

_____

_____

6. _____

_____

_____

7. _____

_____

_____

8. _____

_____

_____

9. _____

_____

_____

_____

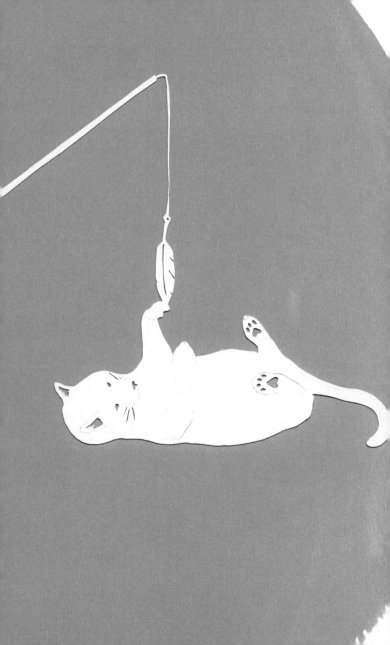

Jot down how hanging out with
your cat makes you feel.

Have you ever caught your cat licking the leftovers off your plate? What does your cat consider a tasty treat?

_____

_____

_____

_____

_____

What would you consider your
cat's best quality to be?

_____

_____

_____

If you could give three quick tips
to a brand-new cat owner,
what would they be?

1. _____

_____

_____

_____

2. _____

_____

_____

_____

3. _____

_____

_____

_____

Kittens are angels with whiskers.

AUTHOR UNKNOWN

CONGRATULATIONS!

You've reached the tail end of the book!

You know your pet was special, but until you recorded all these memories, you probably didn't quite realize how much richer life is with a cat.

And there's no need to stop here. You can return to these pages and jot down more memories and stories and fun facts. You can even start your own memory journal or keepsake scrapbook—maybe one that includes all of your cats or other animals—using this book for ideas and inspiration.

Now, take a cue from your cat. Hang out, relax, and soak in the comfort of everyday pleasures. You know, like having a cat cuddle up on your lap.

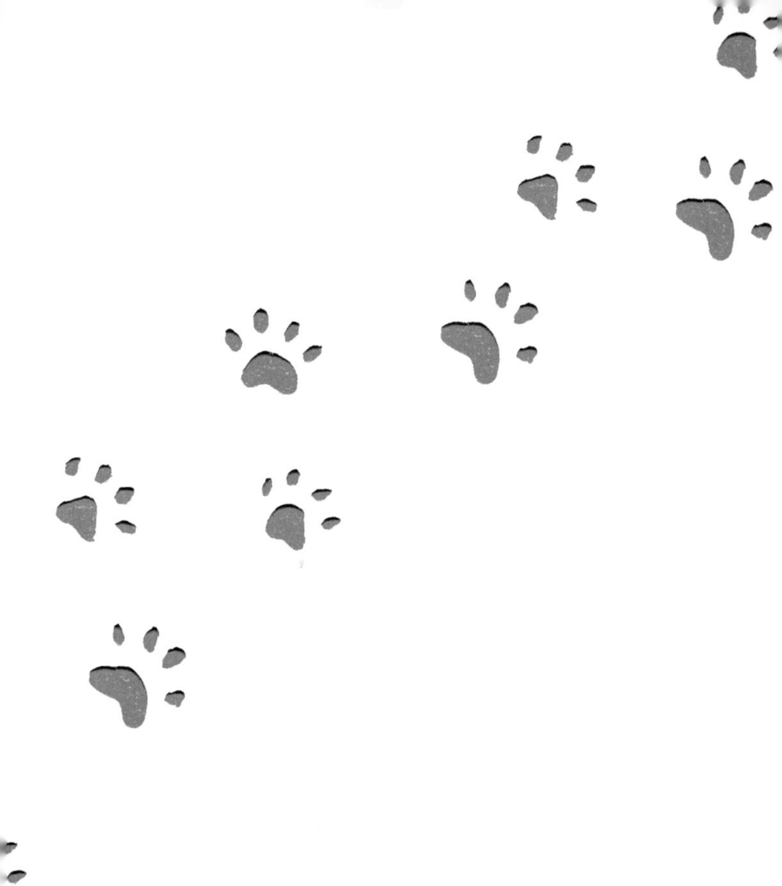